Texas Cookoff

by Carol Blakely

Edited by: Jeanne Wright, Dwayne and Joan Liffring-Zug
Dorothy Crum, Melinda Bradnan, and Kathleen Timm
Cover design: Molly Cook, M.A. Cook Design
Historic Texas postcards from the collection of Carol B
Drawings by Diane Heusinkveld

Stewing in Texas

Texas Cookoff contains a selection of recipes from the book *Stewing in Texas*, the exciting tale of a landmark copyright case in 2001–2002. Carol Blakely contributed great Texas recipes to this earlier Penfield book that tells the hilarious story of a lawsuit—involving eighteen recipes and huge legal costs. Blakely's research and resourcefulness helped solve the case, proving once again that Blakely is one of the leading authorities on southwestern cooking. (See Books by Mail on page 165, for *Stewing in Texas* and other titles.)

ISBN 1-932043-39-X   ©2007 Penfield Books

The Author

Texas native, cook extraordinaire, culinary historian, computer expert, and a feisty grandmother, Carol Blakely of Dallas is a serious "foodie" and cookbook collector. A former systems consultant for a software company, Carol shares her love of cooking with her retired military husband, Ralph, their three adult children, and five grandchildren. She also runs *The Jalapeño Café*, www.jalapenocafe.com, a website with monthly recipe updates and a cooking newsletter with subscribers from around the world. Her favorite type of cuisine is Southwestern.

An unshared recipe will soon be forgotten, but a shared recipe will live forever.

—From an old community cookbook

Contents

The Author 3

Appetizers 5–22

Salads, Sauces, Soups, & Main
    Dishes 23–97

Breads & Peppers 98–110

Sweet Stuff 111–144

Drinks 145–155

Cookoffs in Texas 156–159

Index of Recipes 160–164

Peach

Pepper

Appetizers

In Mexican culture, serving *anjojitos* (little whims) or appetizers before a meal is a long-standing tradition. This custom is why you are served corn chips and salsa in a Mexican restaurant while you are waiting for your meal.

Pico de Gallo (Rooster's Beak) is the name for a common Mexican table relish. The name comes from the fact that the relish is hot and will "peck" when eaten. In the southern part of Mexico, it is made with oranges, jicama, and chili powder. The jicama is a crunchy root vegetable that tastes like a cross between a potato and an apple. In Northern Mexico, in the cattle-raising states, Pico de Gallo is made with tomatoes, onions, and jalapeño peppers. The northern version is a popular accompaniment to fajitas.

Pico de Gallo One (Rooster's Beak)

3 cups chopped jicama
2 cups chopped oranges
2 limes, juiced

Salt to taste
Piquin chili powder to taste
   (or any hot chili powder)

Combine the jicama and oranges. Add the lime juice and salt to taste. Mix well; chill for 2 to 3 hours. Just before serving sprinkle lightly with the chili powder.

Pico de Gallo Two (Rooster's Beak)

4 or 5 ripe plum or Roma tomatoes,
   finely chopped
1 small onion, finely chopped
2 or 3 fresh jalapeños, chopped (for less heat, remove seeds and white membrane)

1/4 cup fresh, chopped cilantro
Juice of two limes
1 teaspoon salt

Mix ingredients; chill for 1 hour before serving.

Easy Skillet Fajitas

4 chicken breasts, halved
Juice of 2 limes
2 teaspoons garlic powder
4 tablespoons Worcestershire sauce
2 tablespoons salad or olive oil

1 large onion, sliced in rounds
1 large bell pepper, top and membrane removed, sliced in rings
Salt and pepper to taste

Trim fat from chicken and slice lengthwise into thin pieces. Mix lime juice, garlic powder, Worcestershire sauce, and oil; pour over chicken, coating well. Let stand 15 to 20 minutes. Heat heavy skillet and spray with non-stick spray. Remove chicken from marinade and place on hot skillet to cook. Add the sliced vegetables to the leftover marinade to soak while the chicken cooks. Turn chicken to ensure it

(continued)

is cooked throughout, 6 to 8 minutes. Add the vegetables and cook a few minutes more. Season with salt and pepper. Heap on hot platter to serve. Serve with hot flour tortillas, Pico de Gallo, sour cream, guacamole, refried beans, and lime slices.

Easy way to heat tortillas: Lay eight tortillas flat and wrap paper towels around them. Microwave on high for 60 seconds. Let stand a minute to finish heating through.

Olive branch

Prairie Fire One

4 tablespoons butter
1 onion, finely grated
1 garlic clove, finely minced
1 can Ranch-Style Beans™
 (or chili beans)

2 pickled jalapeño peppers, minced, plus 2 or 3 tablespoons of the jalapeño juice
1 cup grated Cheddar cheese

Melt butter in skillet. Add onion and cook until limp. Add garlic and cook 1 minute longer, then add beans. Mash beans with potato masher as they cook. Add the jalapeños and juice, mixing well. Turn heat to low and add cheese, stirring to melt. Serve the dip in a chafing dish with tortilla chips.

Prairie Fire Two

1 can refried beans
1 (4-ounce) can chopped
    green chilies
1 teaspoon garlic salt

1/4 cup butter
2 pickled jalapeños, minced
1 cup grated Cheddar cheese

Place refried beans, green chilies, garlic salt, butter, and jalapeños in heavy pan or skillet and cook on medium heat until warm, adding a little water if needed. Turn heat to low and add cheese, stirring to mix. Serve with tortilla chips.

Note: This recipe can be made in the microwave, covering the first mixture with waxed paper and cooking on high 3 minutes, then stirring and cooking 2 minutes more. Add cheese and cook on low 1 minute.

Lady Bird Johnson's Cheese Wafers

2 sticks (1 cup) butter
1 pound sharp Cheddar cheese, grated
1 teaspoon cayenne pepper
Dash salt
2 cups flour
2 cups plain Rice Krispies™

Place butter in bowl and mix with grated cheese to soften at room temperature. When softened, add cayenne and salt to flour. Add flour mixture to cheese mixture. This can be done with a food processor or mixer, but add Rice Krispies™ by hand. Drop by small rounds on a greased cookie sheet. Press with the back of the spoon to flatten. Bake at 350° for 10 to 12 minutes until lightly browned. Makes 60 wafers.

Old-fashioned Cheese Dollars

1/2 cup butter
1 cup grated sharp Cheddar cheese
2 (3-ounce) packages cream
    cheese, softened
Pecan halves

2-1/4 cups flour
1 teaspoon cayenne pepper
1/8 teaspoon salt
1 teaspoon white pepper

Cream butter and cheeses together until cheese is thoroughly incorporated. Mix in remaining ingredients. Divide dough into two equal parts and shape each part into a long roll about 2 inches across. Wrap rolls in waxed paper and chill until firm (2 hours or more). To bake, slice into 1/4-inch thick rounds and place on ungreased cookie sheet. Press a pecan half in the center of each "dollar." Bake in 350° oven 10 to 12 minutes until lightly browned. Makes 70 to 80. (These wafers store well in an airtight container.)

Armadillo Eggs

2 cups Bisquick™
1 pound bulk sausage
    (room temperature)
2 cups shredded Cheddar cheese

2 jars whole jalapeño peppers
1 cup shredded Monterey Jack cheese
1 package Shake 'N Bake™ for pork

Mix Bisquick™, sausage, and Cheddar cheese by hand. Remove stems from peppers and slice lengthwise. Stuff the peppers with the Monterey Jack cheese. Pat small pieces of the Bisquick™ mixture flat and wrap around the stuffed peppers.

    Roll each one in the Shake 'N Bake™. Place on ungreased cookie sheet and bake in 425° oven for 15 to 20 minutes. Makes 20 to 30 "eggs."

GUACAMOLE

Over the years, I have made guacamole hundreds of times and used many different recipes. Almost all were good, but I have come to some conclusions about guacamole. The basic ingredients that must be in the guacamole (besides the avocado) are tomato, garlic, salt, and lime juice. I like to use fresh garlic, but have used garlic powder in a pinch. The addition of any type of green chile is good, as well as onion and cilantro.

The old story about placing the seed in the dish to keep the avocado from turning brown is simply not true. The only way to keep leftover guacamole from darkening is to squeeze a little lemon or lime juice over the top of the mixture, then cover and store in refrigerator. It will be green the next day.

Perfect Guacamole

2 large or 3 medium-sized ripe avocados, peeled and deseeded
1 small ripe plum tomato
1 or 2 cloves of garlic, mashed
1 teaspoon salt or salt to taste
Juice of 1 lime combined with the salt

Mash avocado with fork until almost smooth, leaving a few lumps for texture. Slice the end off the tomato and grate the pulp into the avocado mixture; discard the tomato skin. Add the mashed garlic and salt/lime juice, mixing well. Chill in the refrigerator 15 to 20 minutes before serving.

Poo Poos

12 ounces sharp Cheddar cheese, grated
1 pound pork sausage (hot preferred)
3 cups Bisquick™
2 tablespoons finely chopped, pickled jalapeños

Put ingredients in a bowl and let stand for 15 or 20 minutes to reach room temperature. Mix thoroughly by hand. Allow the mixture to rest for 15 to 20 minutes. Form the dough into 1-inch balls. Place on an ungreased cookie sheet and bake in 350° oven 10 to 12 minutes until lightly browned. Yield will be about 100 Poo Poos.

Guacamole Dip

Avocado

3 or 4 large ripe avocados, peeled and deseeded
1 small ripe tomato, peeled and finely chopped
1 (4-ounce) can chopped green chilies
2 tablespoons finely chopped onion
1 pickled jalapeño, finely chopped (for heat lovers only)
1 or 2 garlic cloves, mashed with 1 teaspoon salt
Juice of 1 lime

Place avocados in bowl and mash with fork until almost smooth. Leave a few lumps for texture. Add the other ingredients and mix well. Serve at once with corn chips.

Texas Caviar (with black olives)

1 pound fresh green beans
2 ripe tomatoes, chopped
1 can whole ripe black olives
    (without seeds)
1 Texas sweet onion (Noonday or
    1015 preferred), cut into rings

Dressing:
3/4 cup extra-virgin olive oil
3 tablespoons lemon juice
2 cloves garlic, finely minced
1 teaspoon Dijon mustard
1 teaspoon salt
1/2 teaspoon fresh cracked pepper

Clean beans, removing stems and ends. Cook about 5 minutes in salted boiling water. Drain and place in ice water to stop cooking. When cool, drain and chill until ready to use.

To make salad, place green beans, tomatoes, olives, and onion in large bowl. Mix dressing ingredients and pour over salad. Toss lightly to mix and chill about 15 minutes before serving. Great with fried chicken and barbeque.

Onion

Black-eyed Pea Dip or Salad

2 (16-ounce) cans black-eyed peas,
    drained
1 small onion, diced
2 ripe plum tomatoes, chopped
1 green (or red) bell pepper, diced
3 or 4 stalks celery, finely diced
2 to 3 tablespoons finely chopped
    jalapeño peppers
2 (4-ounce) cans chopped black
    olives, drained

Dressing:
3/4 cup extra virgin olive oil
1/4 cup wine vinegar
1/4 teaspoon dry mustard
1 teaspoon garlic salt
1/2 teaspoon fresh cracked ground
    pepper
2 teaspoons Tabasco™ sauce

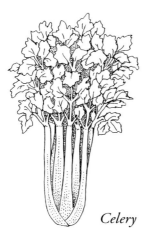

Celery

Mix salad ingredients in large bowl. In small bowl, mix dressing ingredients and pour over pea mixture, tossing to mix. Cover and let stand in refrigerator 4 to 5 hours or overnight. Serve with tostado corn chips.

Jalapeño Café Snack Mix

3/4 cup butter (1-1/2 sticks)
6 tablespoons Worcestershire sauce
2 tablespoons Tabasco™ sauce
1/2 teaspoon garlic powder
6 to 8 cups Wheat Chex™, Corn
   Chex™, Cheerios™, or any like cereal

1 teaspoon sage
2 cups tiny pretzel squares
2 cups tiny cheese crackers
2 cups peanuts
1 cup sunflower seeds

Pour melted butter into a large shallow baking pan. Add Worcestershire, Tabasco™, garlic powder, and sage, mixing well. Combine dry ingredients and add to mixture; toss to coat. Bake in 250° oven for 1 hour, stirring every 10 to 15 minutes. Spread on paper towels to cool.

Salads, Sauces, Soups & Main Dishes

Dinner in the Cow Camp

Frito™ Pie

One single-serving-sized bag of Fritos™
1/2 cup warm chili con carne
1 or 2 tablespoons chopped onion
1 or 2 tablespoons grated Cheddar cheese
Additional toppings: chopped avocado, ripe black olives, finely diced tomato,
    pickled jalapeño slices

Press on sealed bag to slightly crunch Fritos™, then make lengthwise slit along edge of bag. Spoon in chili; top with onion, cheese, and other toppings. Eat from bag with plastic spoon.

Frito™ Enchilada Pie

3 cups small-size Fritos™ corn chips
1 (16-ounce) can chili with beans
1 small onion, finely chopped
1 cup grated Cheddar cheese
1 small (4-ounce) can sliced black olives

Onion

Spray a 9 x 9-inch glass baking dish with non-stick cooking spray. Place Fritos™ in dish; crunch chips slightly with a large spoon or spatula. Spoon chili over Fritos™ and sprinkle with chopped onion. Top with grated cheese and spread black olives on top. Bake in 425° oven 15 minutes or long enough to warm the chili and melt the cheese.

Oven Barbeque Brisket

1 large (5 to 6 pound) beef brisket
3 teaspoons seasoning salt
1 teaspoon pepper
2 teaspoons garlic powder

3 tablespoons Worcestershire sauce
3 tablespoons liquid smoke
2 or 3 bay leaves

Preheat oven to 450°. Trim excess fat from meat and place in roasting pan. Rub seasoning salt, pepper, and garlic powder over meat. Shake Worcestershire sauce and liquid smoke all over meat. Add the bay leaves. Let cook uncovered 15 minutes. Cover meat and reduce oven temperature to 250°. Bake 5 to 6 hours or until tender, basting often. If meat is dry, add a little more Worcestershire sauce or

liquid smoke. The last 30 minutes, remove cover and increase heat to 425° to crisp up outside of meat. Remove from oven and allow to stand 15 minutes. Slice and serve with pinto beans and Texas Potato Salad.

Good for leftovers, too. This meat makes great filling for enchiladas and tacos.

A Texas steer

A BOWL OF RED

Nothing says "Texas" more than a bowl of steaming hot chili. The origins of this fiery stew are hotly debated by chili aficionados. Some say it originated on the cattle drives in South Texas, where the chuck-wagon cooks plucked wild chili pepper to add to their stews. Others say it originated in San Antonio, where the Chili Queens served the dish on plank tables in the open plazas for almost a hundred years. Another tale is that it originated in the county jails with the chilies used to disguise the taste of cheap, inferior cuts of meat. In 1977, the Texas legislature designated chili as the official state dish. As long as you have some meat and chilies, you can produce this dish; the other ingredients are left up to your imagination. Chili was a cheap dish to feed to the prisoners in the Texas jails of long ago. The jail keeper brought home a deer or some other game meat, and his wife cooked up the stew using the spices she had on hand.

Pioneer Jailhouse Chili

1/4 cup lard or shortening
3 pounds coarse ground meat (beef, pork, venison, possum, squirrel)
1 tablespoon cayenne pepper
2 tablespoons ground cumin
6 to 8 tablespoons chili powder
3 tablespoons sweet pepper (paprika)
8 cloves garlic, finely minced
2 tablespoons salt
1 tablespoon black pepper
1 quart water
3 tablespoons flour
3 tablespoons cornmeal

Heat lard in heavy skillet; add meat and cook until it turns gray. Add other ingredients, except flour and cornmeal, and cook 2 more minutes. Add 1 quart of water and bring to a boil. Reduce heat and simmer 2-1/2 to 3 hours, adding more

(continued)

water if needed. Mix 3 tablespoons flour and 3 tablespoons cornmeal with enough water to make a thin paste. Add to chili, stirring constantly. Cook for another 15 to 20 minutes, stirring to keep from burning.

A Texas corncob

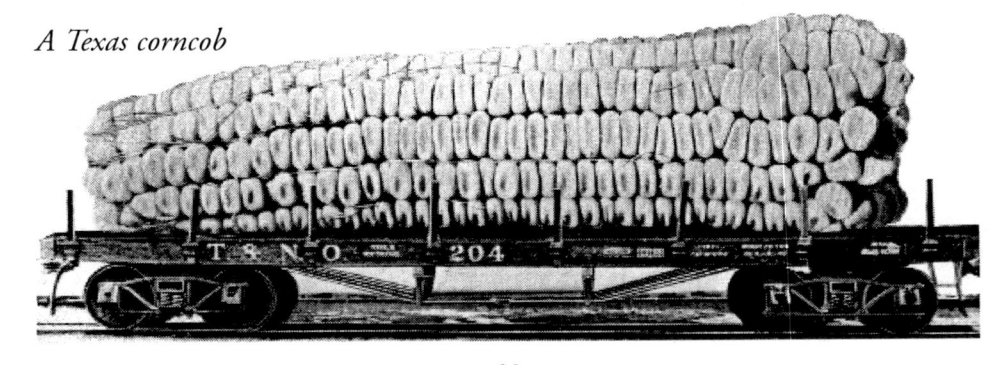

Classic Texas Chili

- 2 tablespoons oil
- 2-1/2 to 3 pounds beef (chuck or stew meat), cut into small pieces
- 4 to 5 tablespoons chili powder
- 1 tablespoon cayenne pepper
- 1 heaping tablespoon ground cumin
- 1 onion, chopped
- 1 teaspoon dried oregano (Mexican preferred)
- 4 cloves garlic, minced
- 1 (15-ounce) can tomato sauce
- 3 tablespoons masa harina or cornmeal

Heat oil in skillet and cook meat until it is gray. Place meat in heavy pan and add other ingredients except the masa meal. Pour in enough water to cover the meat to a depth of 2 inches. Bring the mixture to a boil, then reduce heat, cover, and

(continued)

simmer for 2-1/2 to 3 hours or until meat is tender. Add more water as needed. Make a thin paste with the masa meal and water. Add to chili, mixing well. Let simmer another 30 minutes; taste the chili and correct the seasoning. Letting the chili stand overnight in the refrigerator improves the flavor.

When ready to serve, warm up the chili, put on some Bob Wills Texas swing, get some cold long-necks and soda crackers, and invite your friends over to share your meal.

Pinto Beans

Pinto beans are a staple in Texas cooking, and I wouldn't dream of having a barbeque without pinto beans on the menu. When you cook beans they should never go to waste as the leftovers can be made into *Frijoles Refritos* (refried beans) or delicious creamy Pinto Bean Soup.

The following recipe is for flavorful beans, seasoned with jalapeños, tomatoes, and cilantro.

Tomatoes

Charro Beans (Cowboy Beans)

1 (1 pound) bag pinto beans
1 small onion, chopped
4 slices bacon, cut into quarters, or chopped ham (optional)
4 ripe plum tomatoes or 2 medium-sized tomatoes, chopped
4 or 5 fresh jalapeño peppers, stems removed, coarsely chopped
4 cloves garlic, minced
1 boullion cube
1/3 cup chopped cilantro

Rinse beans under hot water for a few minutes to soften. Place beans in large pan, adding onion, bacon or ham, chopped tomato, jalapeño, and garlic. Cover with water and bring to a boil. Reduce heat and cover. Simmer on low 2-1/2 to 3 hours, adding water as needed. Cook until beans are soft. When beans are almost cooked, add boullion cube and the chopped cilantro. Let cool 10 to 15 minutes longer. Served with warm flour tortillas and salsa, it's a meal in itself. Great with grilled steaks, too.

Chuck wagon cowboy kitchen

Jalapeño Café Enchilada Casserole

1 pound lean ground beef
1 small onion, chopped
1 or 2 cloves garlic, chopped
Salt and pepper to taste

12 corn tortillas
1 large can (14-ounce) or 2 small
    cans enchilada sauce
1 cup grated Cheddar or Cheddar/
    Jack cheese
1 can sliced ripe olives, drained

Brown the ground beef in a heavy skillet with the onions, cooking until the meat is browned and the onions clear. Add the chopped garlic and cook a minute or two more. Season to taste with salt and pepper. Set aside.

Soften the corn tortillas, either by dipping in oil or by spraying both sides with a non-stick spray, wrapping in a paper towel and putting in the microwave for 60 seconds. Cut the softened tortillas in quarters and set aside.

Open the can of enchilada sauce and pour in bowl. Spray a small casserole dish (8 x 8-inch) with non-stick spray.

Take 1/3 of the tortillas and dip them in the sauce and then lay them in the casserole dish, spreading out so the bottom is covered. Spoon 1/3 of the meat on top and spoon a little sauce on the meat. Repeat the process until the tortillas and meat are gone. Pour any leftover enchilada sauce over the meat. Sprinkle the ripe olives on top and then cover with the grated cheese.

Bake in a 425° oven about 15 to 20 minutes until hot and bubbling and the cheese is melted. Serves 4 to 6.

Pinto Bean Soup

A great way to use leftover pinto beans. Canned beans can be used, but are less flavorful than day-old home-cooked beans.

1 tablespoon oil
1 large onion, chopped
1 clove garlic, minced
3 cups cooked leftover beans with liquid

6 cups chicken stock
Salt to taste
Dash of Tabasco™ sauce

Garnishes:
Corn tortillas, cut into thin strips and fried crisp
Avocado, chopped

Monterey Jack cheese, cut into small chunks
Pico de Gallo
Lime slices

Heat oil in heavy skillet. Add onions and stir. Cook on medium heat until brown and caramelized (10 to 15 minutes). Add garlic and cook 1 minute more. Place beans and onion mixture in food processor and process until smooth and creamy.

    Place bean mixture in soup pot and add chicken stock. Salt the soup and add a shake of hot sauce. If too thick, thin with bean liquid or stock until a cream-like consistency. Let soup simmer on low 15 minutes. Serve with garnishes. Leftover beans improve in flavor after a day or so in the refrigerator.

Frijoles Refritos (Refried Beans)

1/4 cup oil or bacon drippings
1 small onion, chopped
3 cloves garlic, minced

3 cups cooked leftover pinto beans,
    plus 1 cup of cooking liquid
Salt to taste
Grated Monterey Jack or Cheddar
    cheese (optional)

Heat oil in skillet. Add onion and garlic and fry until softened, about 3 minutes. Add the beans and mash with potato masher while stirring in a little bean liquid at a time. Continue mashing and stirring and add enough liquid to reach a smooth consistency. Season mixture with salt. You can sprinkle a little cheese on top.

Maggie's Hot Cheese Toasts

This recipe, from Maggie Jacobson, makes delicious cheese toasts that go well with soup.

8 slices bacon
1/3 cup mayonnaise
1 cup shredded sharp Cheddar cheese
1 small onion, grated
1 egg, lightly beaten
Fresh ground pepper
1/2 teaspoon Worcestershire sauce
Several dashes Tabasco™ sauce
8 slices white bread

Cook bacon. Drain and set aside. When cool, crumble bacon. Combine all ingredients, except bread in a bowl and mix well. Cut crust from bread and toast on both sides. Spread each slice with mixture, then cut into 3 strips. Sprinkle with paprika. Place toast strips on cookie sheet and bake in 350° oven for about 20 minutes, or until lightly browned and puffy. Serve hot.

Sweet and Spicy Shrimp

3/4 cup apple jelly
1/3 cup fresh lime juice
1 tablespoon Worcestershire sauce

1 fresh jalapeño pepper, minced fine
2 pounds large shrimp, shelled and
    deveined
Salt to taste

Prepare 12-inch wooden skewers by soaking in water for 45 minutes before using.

Combine jelly, lime juice, Worcestershire sauce, and jalapeño pepper in small saucepan. Cook over medium heat until the jelly dissolves. Remove from heat to cool.

Thread four shrimp on each wooden skewer so shrimp will lay flat. Brush both sides of shrimp with jelly mixture, coating well. Place on tray and allow to marinate for 15 minutes. Just before grilling, salt to taste. Grill shrimp 2 minutes on each side, brushing on more of the jelly mixture before turning. Serve hot on skewers with remaining sauce. Serves 6 to 8.

Note: You can substitute boneless chicken breast, cut into strips. Place one strip on each skewer. Increase cooking time on grill.

Lime slices

Texas Shrimp Gumbo

Texans love gumbo as much as the Louisiana Cajuns. There is a little difference in the recipe; Texans add okra to their version.

2 cups fresh sliced okra or
    1 package frozen okra
1/4 cup oil
1 medium-sized onion, chopped
3 cloves garlic, finely minced
1-1/2 teaspoons salt

1/2 teaspoon pepper
2 pounds raw shrimp, peeled and
    deveined
2 cans diced tomatoes
2 bay leaves
1 teaspoon Tabasco™ sauce
3 cups cooked rice

Sauté okra in oil about 10 minutes, stirring constantly. Add onion, garlic, salt, pepper, and shrimp. Cook 5 minutes. Add tomatoes and bay leaves; cover and simmer 15 minutes. Remove bay leaves and add Tabasco™ sauce. Let stand 5 or 10 minutes. Place 1/2 cup rice in bottom of six soup bowls; fill with gumbo.

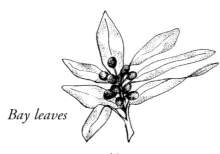

Bay leaves

Baked Potato Chowder

The potato chowder in restaurants is usually bland tasting like mashed potatoes. Here's a recipe that has plenty of flavor. The amounts can grow or shrink according to how many people you will be feeding and how many leftover potatoes you have on hand. This soup tastes even better warmed over.

6 strips of bacon
1 onion, chopped
2 stalks of celery, chopped
1/2 cup frozen corn
3 large leftover baked potatoes, peeled and cubed

2 cans of chicken stock
2 cups of milk
2 teaspoons Tabasco™ sauce
Salt and pepper to taste

Fry the bacon until crisp in skillet. Drain on paper towels and crumble into small bits. Drain off all the bacon grease in the skillet except 1 tablespoon, and brown onion and celery in hot grease. Cook until soft.

In large saucepan, add crumbled bacon, celery and onions, corn, cubed potatoes, chicken stock, and enough milk to make right consistency. Add salt, pepper, and Tabasco™. Heat over medium high, stirring often; bring to boil, turn down and simmer for 15 minutes. Taste and correct the seasoning.

If you like a thicker soup, you can add a few tablespoons of flour thinned in water, then stirred into the soup and cooked a few more minutes.

Split Pea Soup — Slow Cooker Method

Split peas get bad press, starting with the old nursery rhyme "Peas Porridge Hot," but they make tasty soup. By using a slow cooker or CrockPot™, you can put the ingredients on to simmer and not have to "watch the pot" as the soup cooks.

1 pound package split peas
1 large onion, chopped
2 stalks celery, chopped
3 carrots, scraped and chopped
Ham hock or two chicken wings
    (meat can be omitted)

Stock or water to cover
Milk and/or water as needed to thin
    soup
Salt and pepper to taste
2 tablespoons Tabasco™ sauce
4 pieces fried crisp bacon, crumbled
    (optional)

Rinse peas in colander under hot water. Add to slow cooker along with onion, celery, carrots, and ham hock or chicken pieces. Cook on high until peas are cooked soft, about 3 or 4 hours. Remove ham hock or chicken wings. Take meat from bones, cut into small pieces and add back to soup. Mash mixture with potato masher until almost smooth, leave a few lumps for texture. Thin with water or milk to a good consistency, like a thin gravy. Add Tabasco™ sauce and correct the seasoning with salt and pepper. Add the crumbled bacon and simmer for 15 minutes longer. Garnish with garlic croutons or toasted bread cubes.

Peas

CHICKEN

Cherokee chicken is not a true Native-American dish, because it uses chicken, a domestic bird. But when different cultures meet, as happened with the settling of America, one result is the exchange of foods and recipes. Hominy is an Indian food, which was adapted by early immigrants and became a food staple on southern tables. The American Indians changed their eating habits as new food sources became available. A good example of an adapted Cherokee Indian food is frybread, using wheat flour with baking powder, salt and water to form a dough. The dough was kneaded and formed into balls and fried in hot oil. For special occasions, the Cherokees used to cook up quail or other game birds with dried berries. Here is a modernized version of this dish, using chicken and cranberries.

Cherokee Chicken

1/4 cup vegetable oil
3 tablespoons butter
2 pounds boneless chicken breast,
    cut into serving-sized pieces
1 green pepper, chopped

2 cloves garlic, minced
1/3 cup chopped onion
1 can whole cranberry sauce
Salt and pepper to taste

Heat oil and butter in a heavy skillet. Add chicken pieces and cook until brown on all sides. Remove from skillet as browned. Pour off all but 2 tablespoons of the oil mixture. Add green pepper, garlic, and onion. Cook until soft. Add cranberry sauce, salt, and pepper, mixing well. Add chicken back to skillet; cover and simmer 30 minutes or until done.

Cerise Chicken

Here is another version of chicken cooked with fruit. This recipe comes from Georgia, part of the Cherokees' original homeland.

1 (2 pound) chicken, cut into
    serving pieces
Paprika and salt
6 tablespoons butter
1 tablespoon flour
1 teaspoon sugar
1/8 teaspoon ground allspice
1/8 teaspoon ground cinnamon

1/8 teaspoon dry mustard
1 teaspoon salt
2 cups canned, water-packed,
    pitted, red sour cherries
1 (small) can crushed pineapple
1 chicken boullion cube
1 teaspoon red food coloring

Season chicken with paprika and salt. Sauté chicken in butter until brown. Remove chicken. Blend in flour, sugar, spices, and 1 teaspoon salt in butter remaining in skillet. Drain cherries and pour the liquid into the skillet. Return chicken to skillet. Add pineapple, boullion cube, and food coloring. Cover; simmer 30 minutes. Add cherries and cook 10 minutes more. To serve, arrange chicken on a bed of rice. Spoon some sauce over chicken and serve the remaining sauce separately.

Pineapple

King Ranch Chicken

This famous casserole was named for the King Ranch, the largest ranch in Texas. It covers three counties and more than 825,000 acres of Gulf coastal plains. The ranch has its own breed of cattle, Santa Gertrudis, and is dotted with oil wells. According to local legend, this recipe was created by the Mexican cooks on the ranch who had to prepare huge meals for the cowboys and oil-field workers. One thing is for sure: this recipe will feed a lot of people. In Texas, the recipe is made with Rotel™ tomatoes, a local brand of canned tomatoes with hot green chilies. If not available, use plain canned tomatoes and add green chilies, plus a few chopped jalapeños.

1 (3 to 4 pound) large chicken
Herbs, onion, or celery, to season
1 large onion, chopped
1 chopped bell pepper
2 tablespoons oil
2 cloves garlic, finely minced
1 can cream of mushroom soup
1 can cream of chicken soup
    (optional)
2 teaspoon chili powder
Salt and pepper to taste
1 tablespoon Tabasco™ hot sauce
1 can Rotel™ brand tomatoes
2 to 3 finely diced pickled jalapeños
1 package (18 to 20) corn tortillas
2 cups grated longhorn Cheddar
    cheese

Place chicken in large pan and cover with water. Season with herbs, onion, or celery and simmer until meat is tender. Remove chicken, reserving chicken stock. Remove meat from bones and discard skin and bones. Chop meat into

(continued)

bite-sized pieces. Sauté onions and bell peppers in oil until soft, add garlic, and cook a few minutes more. Place in large bowl. Add soups, chicken stock, chili powder, salt and pepper, hot sauce, and Rotel™ tomatoes. Mix well.

Heat stock and dip corn tortillas to soften. Cut or tear tortillas into large pieces and make a layer in bottom of a greased 3-quart casserole dish. Add a layer of half the chopped chicken; spoon on half the soup mixture. Make another tortilla layer, then another layer with the rest of the chicken, and layer with the remainder of the soup mixture. Another thin layer of softened tortillas can be added. Top with the grated cheese. Bake in 350° oven for 35 to 45 minutes. Serves 8 to 10 hungry people.

Squash Dressing

When yellow squash starts making in the garden, you will be looking for different ways to serve it. Here's an unusual recipe, using the squash in a cornbread dressing dish. It goes great with roast chicken.

3 cups chopped yellow squash, cooked
3 cups cornbread, crumbled
3 eggs, beaten
1/3 cup celery, chopped
1/3 cup onion, chopped
2 teaspoons poultry seasoning
Salt and pepper to taste
1 can cream of chicken soup
1/2 stick butter
Little milk or water, if dressing is too dry

Mix all ingredients except butter and place in greased baking dish. Dot top with small pats of butter. Bake at 350° for 1 hour.

Sonora Chicken Pie

Years ago, the Texas Electric Company included a recipe folder with their monthly electric bill. This recipe was in one of those folders. It is easy to make and a surefire pleaser. You can find salsa verde *in the Mexican food section of your supermarket.*

6 cups cubed cooked chicken
12 ounces *salsa verde* (Mexican green sauce)
2 cups sour cream

1 dozen corn tortillas, cut into 1-1/2–inch pieces
1-1/2 pound Monterey Jack cheese, shredded

Arrange half the chicken pieces in a lightly greased 9 x 13-inch baking dish. Spread half the *salsa verde* over chicken and half the sour cream. Top with half of the tortilla pieces and half of the cheese. Repeat the layers, using remaining chicken, *salsa verde*, sour cream, and tortillas, ending with the cheese.

Cover dish with foil. (Can be refrigerated overnight, if desired.) Bake, covered in 375° oven for 40 minutes. Uncover and bake an additional 8 minutes or until cheese is bubbly and casserole is hot throughout.

Let stand 10 minutes before serving. To serve, cut into squares. Makes 8 to 12 servings.

SUGAR FRYING

The cooking method of adding sugar to hot oil when browning chicken originated in Africa. African slaves, shipped to the New World to work on the sugar plantations, brought their foods and recipes with them, including the sugar-frying method. Sugar-fried Chicken is a popular Caribbean dish.

Sugar-fried Chicken

2 to 2-1/2 pounds boneless
  chicken breast

Make a marinade of:
1/2 cup catsup
1/2 cup water
1 small onion
3 cloves garlic, minced
1 tablespoon cumin

1/2 cup canola oil
2 tablespoons brown sugar

1 tablespoon Season All™ or
  Old Bay Seasoning™
1 teaspoon pepper
1 teaspoon salt

Coat chicken in marinade and let stand 15 to 20 minutes. Heat the oil in a heavy skillet. Add brown sugar, stirring until melted. Add chicken and brown on both

(continued)

sides. Add the marinade plus 2 cups of water, bring to a boil, and simmer for 20 minutes or until chicken is cooked through. Serve with yellow rice.

Note: To make yellow rice, add 1 teaspoon turmeric to water when cooking rice.

Chickens

Sugar-browned Potatoes

The Danish also use sugar mixed with oil in frying. Here is an old family recipe from Dorthea Whitlock of Roundrock, Texas. Her great-grandmother, born in Copenhagen, Denmark, brought this recipe to Texas over one hundred years ago. Dorthea says her grandmother served this dish with meatballs and red cabbage.

16 small new potatoes	4 tablespoons sugar
4 tablespoons butter	1 teaspoon salt

Cook potatoes in boiling salted water until tender. Allow to cool, then peel, leaving whole. Melt butter in pan or skillet; add sugar, stirring well until sugar is browned. Add the boiled potatoes and cook until browned on all sides. Shake pan frequently to prevent burning. Sprinkle with salt.

CRANBERRIES

Cranberries have been a favorite of Texas cooks for many years. Recipes calling for these fruits are listed in community cookbooks going back to the 1920s. The baked version of cranberry relish seems to have been popular in the Houston area, and it shows up in Texas community cookbooks. I lived in Alaska for over a decade where wild cranberries grow in abundance. I cooked them up into every conceivable concoction: relish, jam, jelly, catsup, nut bread, cookies, sauce, and pie. These red berries are high in vitamins, and their pleasing tart taste perks up an otherwise bland meal. I came upon a recipe using both fresh cranberries and dried cranberries (Craisins™). I am also including two more recipes, one for colorful cranberry punch, which is great for Christmas entertaining. The other is for cranberry catsup, which goes well with venison.

Double Cranberry Relish

1 (16-ounce) bag cranberries
2 bags dried cranberries
  (Craisins™)
1 (14-ounce) can crushed pineapple
  with liquid

1/2 cup sugar
1/2 cup water
2 tablespoons cider vinegar
1/2 teaspoon salt

Mix all ingredients in saucepan and pour into shallow baking dish that has been sprayed with non-stick cooking spray. Bake in 300° oven 45 to 50 minutes, stirring every 15 minutes. This relish goes well with roasted chicken or turkey.

Cranberry Christmas Punch

1 quart Cranberry Juice Cocktail
1 quart Ginger Ale
1 bottle Cold Duck™ (or other red sparkling wine)

Chill all ingredients. Pour into punch bowl and mix. Add an ice ring for a more festive presentation. For more "punch" in the punch, add a cup of vodka.

Cranberry Catsup

I used to make cranberry catsup from high bush cranberries when I lived in North Pole, Alaska. One of my neighbors had given me the recipe, which I misplaced somewhere along the way. Recently I found a recipe for the catsup in the book Norwegian Touches *from Penfield Books. This sauce is great with game meats and poultry dishes.*

1 pound cranberries
1/2 cup mild vinegar
2/3 cup water
1 cup brown sugar
1/2 teaspoon paprika

1 teaspoon cinnamon
1/2 teaspoon cloves
1/2 teaspoon ginger
1/2 teaspoon salt
1/2 teaspoon pepper
2 tablespoons butter

(continued)

Put cranberries, vinegar, and water in pan and boil until cranberries are soft, about 5 minutes. Put through food mill (or process in food processor). Add brown sugar and seasonings and simmer for 3 minutes. Add the butter. Serve at room temperature.

Note: Cranberry catsup can be refrigerated for months.

Historic Texas Cookbook Advice

One danger of overeating—
it may cause you to live beyond your seams.

Don't put off until tomorrow
the things you should have done yesterday.

TEX-MEX ENCHILADAS & TACOS

The Tex-Mex cuisine, so popular in Texas, is a blend of Northern Mexico and South Texas-style foods. The most typical is enchiladas. Here are three enchilada recipes: classic Tex-Mex cheese, beef, and sour cream chicken. If you can't make up your mind, try them all, they are delicious. You can purchase canned enchilada sauce for these recipes, but if you would like to have the real Tex-Mex taste, try making your own chili sauce.

Texas Red Chili Sauce

6 dried red New Mexico-style chilies
6 ancho chilies
Boiling water to cover
3 cloves garlic
3 tablespoons shortening or oil
3 tablespoons flour
1 teaspoon Mexican oregano
2 teaspoons powdered cumin
2 tablespoons rice wine vinegar
2 teaspoons salt

Pull stems from chilies, split open, and remove seeds and white veins. Rinse chilies and place in glass bowl. Cover with boiling water; let stand 30 minutes. Remove from water, reserving liquid. Place chilies in blender or food processor

(continued)

along with garlic cloves. Add 2 cups of the chili liquid. Purée until smooth. Add more liquid if mixture is too thick. Force mixture through strainer to remove bits of chili skin.

In heavy skillet, heat oil or shortening. Add flour, stirring to make a roux. Continue cooking until lightly browned. Add chili mixture, oregano, cumin, vinegar, and salt. Add enough chili liquid to make a thin sauce. Cook on medium low, stirring to keep from burning. Cook until mixture thickens and has the consistency of thin gravy. If too thick, add more chili liquid. This makes enough sauce for two batches of enchiladas.

Sour Cream Chicken Enchiladas

I have eaten so many bad sour cream enchiladas that I came up with my own recipe. If you don't like them hot, omit the jalapeños. If you do like them hot, use 2 tablespoons chopped jalapeños and substitute jalapeño Jack cheese for the cheese.

1 tablespoon salad oil
1/2 cup chopped onion
2 cloves garlic, minced
2 cups chopped cooked chicken
1 tablespoon finely chopped pickled jalapeño (optional)

1 tablespoon juice from pickled jalapeño or 1 tablespoon rice vinegar
1 (4-ounce) can chopped green chilies, divided
1/2 teaspoon salt

(continued)

Sour cream sauce:

2 tablespoons butter
2 tablespoons flour
1-1/4 cups milk

1 cup sour cream
12 ounces Monterey Jack or
    or jalapeño Jack cheese, grated,
    divided

8 to 10 corn tortillas

Make chicken filling:

Heat oil in small skillet and add onion. Cook until limp; add minced garlic and cook 1 or 2 minutes more. Add chicken, chopped jalapeños, pickled jalapeño juice or vinegar, and 1/2 can chopped green chilies; cook until all liquid is absorbed, 3 to 5 minutes. Add 1/2 teaspoon salt or enough to correct the taste. Set mixture aside.

Make sour cream sauce:
Melt butter in skillet; add flour and stir until smooth, taking care to keep from burning. Add milk and stir or whisk until sauce has thickened. Turn off heat before adding sour cream to prevent curdling. Add sour cream, grated cheese, and remaining 1/2 can green chilies, stirring to mix. Add salt to taste.

Prepare tortillas:
Soften corn tortillas by spraying each side of tortilla with non-stick cooking spray. Stack tortillas and wrap in paper towels. Cook in microwave on high for 60 seconds. Tortillas should be soft and roll without breaking.

(continued)

Assemble the enchiladas:

Spray rectangular baking dish with non-stick spray. Spoon enough sour cream sauce in dish to cover bottom.

To make the enchiladas, spoon 2 to 3 tablespoons of the chicken filling on each tortilla, add a little of the grated cheese, and roll up. Lay open side down in the baking dish on top of the sour cream sauce. Continue until all the tortillas are filled and placed in the dish. Pour remaining sour cream sauce over the enchiladas.

Sprinkle remaining Monterey Jack cheese on top. Bake in 425° oven 12 to 15 minutes until the enchiladas are heated through.

Beef Enchiladas

Make enchiladas as described for Sour Cream Chicken Enchiladas, but substitute this filling for the cheese and onion mixture.

2 tablespoons cooking oil	1 (4-ounce) can chopped green chilies
1 small onion, finely minced	1/2 cup red chili sauce
1 clove garlic, chopped	Salt and pepper to taste
2 cups chopped cooked beef	

Heat 2 tablespoons oil in skillet. Add onions and cook until soft. Add garlic and cook a minute longer. Add beef and green chilies and cook, stirring to prevent sticking. Add red chili sauce and season to taste with salt and pepper.

Cheese Enchiladas

1 pound grated longhorn Cheddar
cheese, divided
1 large onion, finely minced
12 corn tortillas

2 to 3 cups homemade red chili
sauce or 2 cans enchilada sauce
1 (small) can sliced black olives
(optional)

Mix half the grated cheese with the minced onion.

Prepare tortillas by spraying each side of the tortilla with non-stick cooking spray. Stack tortillas, place in paper towels, and cook on high in microwave about 60 seconds. The tortillas should be soft enough to be rolled without breaking.

Assemble the enchiladas:
Place about 1/2 cup red sauce in the bottom of large rectangular baking dish that has been sprayed with non-stick cooking spray. Place one tortilla at end of dish; add 2 or 3 tablespoons of the cheese-onion mixture. Roll tortilla up and place open side down in baking dish. Continue making enchiladas until dish is filled. Pour more of the red sauce over enchiladas. Sprinkle with remaining cheese. Sprinkle with black olives on top. Bake in 425° oven 15 to 20 minutes until cheese is melted and sauce is bubbling.

To make restaurant style, place 2 or 3 tablespoons of chili sauce on dinner plate. Place 2 or 3 cheese-filled enchiladas on sauce. Spoon more sauce on enchiladas; top with grated cheese and black olives. If serving refried beans, spoon portion onto serving plate, too. Place plate in microwave and cook on high for 3 minutes or until cheese is melted.

230 Pound Psalm

A little bit of humor from an old Texas church cookbook

Strict is my diet, I must not want. It maketh me to lie down at night hungry.
It leadeth me past the ice cream shop. It trieth my will power.
It leadeth me in the paths of starvation for my figure's sake.
Yea, though I walk through the aisles of the pastry department,
I will buy no sweet rolls. For they are fattening.
The cakes and pies, they tempt me.
Before me is a table with celery and lettuce. My day's quota runneth over.
Surely calories and weight charts shall follow me all the days of my life, and
I shall dwell in the fear of the scales forever.

Ham Tacos

This recipe is a new spin on an old favorite, the Tex-Mex taco. Instead of ground beef, it calls for a filling of cooked ham and potatoes. The tacos are fried to the chewy-crisp stage as preferred in classic Mexican cooking. The filling can also go into store-bought taco shells.

1 small onion, chopped
2 tablespoons vegetable oil
2 cloves garlic, finely minced
1 cup finely chopped ham
1 cup chopped cooked potato
2 teaspoons mild wine vinegar

Salt and pepper to taste
2 teaspoons Worcestershire sauce
8 to 10 corn tortillas
Non-stick cooking spray
Salad oil for frying

(continued)

Serve with:

Shredded iceberg lettuce

Finely chopped tomato

Ranch dressing

2 avocados

Mexican Red Hot™ sauce

Cook onion in 2 tablespoons oil until soft; add garlic and cook 1 minute. Add ham, potato, vinegar, salt, pepper, and Worcestershire sauce. If too dry, add 2 tablespoons water; stir and cook until mixture starts to brown. Remove from heat and prepare tortillas.

Prepare tortillas:

Lightly spray tortillas on each side with non-stick cooking spray. Wrap stacked tortillas in paper towels and microwave on high for 1 minute. The tortillas should be soft and able to be folded without breaking.

Assemble the taco:
Place a little of the ham mixture (about 2 to 3 tablespoons) in the center of each corn tortilla. Press filling together and fold tortilla in half. Continue until all tortillas are filled. Heat about 1 inch of oil in skillet. When hot, carefully lay folded tortilla in oil so filling will not fall out. Let cook on one side and turn and cook on the other. Fry until starting to crisp, but still a little chewy. Drain on paper towels.

Stuff with salad mixture, lay several avocado slices on top, and pass the hot sauce. *Bueno!*

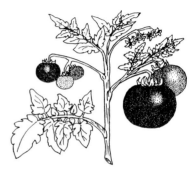

Tomato plant

Sweet Potato Custard

4 cups grated sweet potatoes
3/4 cup brown sugar
1/4 cup molasses
3 tablespoons melted butter
3 eggs, lightly beaten

1/2 teaspoon each of cinnamon,
 cloves, allspice, and ginger
1 teaspoon salt
2 cups milk

Mix all ingredients well and pour into buttered baking dish. Bake at 400° for 40 to 45 minutes.

East Texas Slow Oven Stew

This common recipe from a community cookbook is sometimes called Forgotten Stew.

2 pounds boneless stew meat, cubed
2 or 3 carrots, sliced
1 onion, sliced
1 large potato, cut in small pieces
2 or 3 stalks celery, sliced
1 can cream of mushroom soup plus
    one soup can of water

Salt and pepper to taste
1 bay leaf
1 tablespoon Worcestershire sauce
1 can oven-ready biscuits
    (10 biscuits)

(continued)

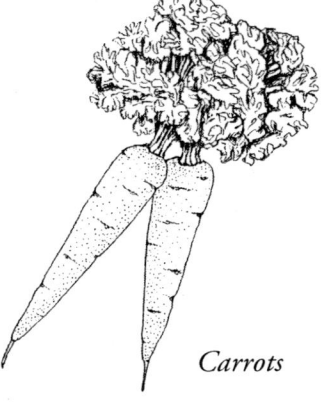

Carrots

Place soup, water, and seasonings in 2-quart baking dish; stir to mix. Add meat and vegetables; stir to coat. (**Note:** To have a brown gravy in the stew, flour the meat and brown in oil before adding to stew ingredients.) Cover baking dish and bake in 275° oven for about 5 hours or until meat is tender. Add a little more water as needed. Remove stew from oven; turn heat up to 375°.

Cut biscuit rounds in quarters and place on top of stew. Return to oven and bake 8 to 10 minutes until biscuits are browned.

South Dallas Short Ribs

This recipe is from a defunct Dallas restaurant, Clara's Kitchen. *People used to come from far and wide to eat Clara's famous soul food.*

2 to 3 pounds beef short ribs

Make the baking sauce:

1 (14-ounce) bottle chili sauce or catsup
1 (12-ounce) can of Coca-Cola™
4 tablespoons Worcestershire sauce
1 teaspoon black pepper
1 teaspoon celery salt
2 tablespoons Louisiana hot sauce

(continued)

Cook short ribs in boiling water about 5 minutes. (This removes excess fat.) Drain and place in baking dish. Pour sauce over meat and cover. Cook at 325°, basting often. Cook for about 2 hours or until meat is falling off bones. Serve with cooked turnip greens, sweet potato custard, and cornbread on the side.

> *If face powder catches a man, then*
> *baking powder keeps him.*
> —Carol Blakely

Macaroni and Cheese Mexicana

2 cups medium elbow macaroni
1/2 cup butter
3 tablespoons flour
1 clove garlic, finely minced
1/2 onion, finely minced
1 teaspoon salt
1/2 teaspoon pepper
3 cups milk
1 (4-ounce) can diced green chilies
1-1/2 cups grated Cheddar cheese
1-1/2 cups Monterey Jack cheese
1 cup crushed tortilla chips
Paprika

Cook macaroni in boiling, salted water until tender but firm. Drain well.

In a medium saucepan, melt the butter, and then add the flour, cooking until smooth, stirring to prevent burning. Add the minced onion, garlic, salt and

(continued)

pepper, and chopped green chilies. Cook, stirring constantly for about 2 minutes. Add milk slowly, stirring or whisking until smooth. Cook over medium heat until thick. Remove from heat. Add the grated cheeses and stir until the cheeses are melted. Correct the salt and pepper seasoning.

Combine the macaroni and cheese sauce. Pour into a 2-1/2 quart casserole. Top with tortilla chips and sprinkle with paprika. Bake at 350° for 25 minutes. Serves 6.

Cabbage Tamales

Meat Filling:

1-1/2 pounds lean ground beef
1 onion, chopped
2 to 3 tablespoons chili powder
1/2 teaspoon pepper
1 tablespoon Worcestershire sauce
1/2 cup Paces Picante Sauce™
1/3 cup cornmeal or masa
1/2 teaspoon salt

Mix meat filling, letting stand for several hours, or overnight in refrigerator improves flavor.

For Tamales:

1 large cabbage, loose leaves
1 can tomato sauce
1 can Rotel™ tomatoes with green chilies

(continued)

Drop cabbage leaves in boiling water, cook until limp (4 to 5 minutes). Drain and when cool enough to handle, cut away heavy stems. Place meat filling in cabbage leaves and roll up, folding ends. Place seam side down in shallow baking dish and pour Rotel™ tomatoes and tomato sauce over all. Cover and bake in 350° oven about 50 minutes until done.

This is also a great slow cooker dish; just place the cabbage tamales in slow cooker and cover with tomatoes.

Cabbage

Texas Goulash

1-1/4 to 1-1/2 pounds lean ground beef
1 onion, chopped
2 or 3 tablespoons chili powder
2 cans tomato sauce
Salt and pepper to taste

2 cups cooked pinto beans, rinsed and drained
1 (8-ounce) package of spaghetti, broken into small pieces, cooked and drained
2 cups grated longhorn Cheddar cheese

Place meat and onion in large skillet. Cook until meat is browned and onions limp. Add the pinto beans and cook and stir until beans are mixed with meat

(continued)

and onions. Add the chili powder and mix well. Add the tomato sauce. Add a little water if the sauce is too dry. Taste and correct seasoning and let simmer a few minutes. Add the cooked spaghetti and mix well.

Pour the mixture into a greased casserole dish and top with the grated cheese. Bake in a 425° oven about 15 minutes, until the cheese is melted and lightly browned on top. Serves 6 to 8 people.

Wyatt's Cafeteria Eggplant Casserole

This recipe comes from a chain of cafeterias that operated in Texas for many years until closing in the 1990s. Wyatt's was famous for this recipe and with good reason. It's a tasty dish. The little touch of sage is the perfect addition to the vegetable flavors.

1 small eggplant
4 ounces dry white bread
1 cup evaporated milk
1/4 cup onion, chopped
1/4 cup green bell pepper, chopped
1/4 cup celery, chopped
3 tablespoons butter, melted
1 tablespoon chopped pimento
1 egg, beaten
1 teaspoon sage
1/2 teaspoon each salt and pepper
1 firm tomato, thinly sliced
4 ounces Cheddar cheese, grated

(continued)

Soak eggplant overnight in salt water. Boil until done; drain. Soak bread in milk. Sauté onion, celery, and bell pepper in butter. Combine eggplant, bread, sautéed vegetables, pimento, egg, and seasonings. Mix well. Pour half into greased baking dish, add layers of sliced tomato. Repeat layer. Top with cheese and bake in 375° oven about 20 to 25 minutes.

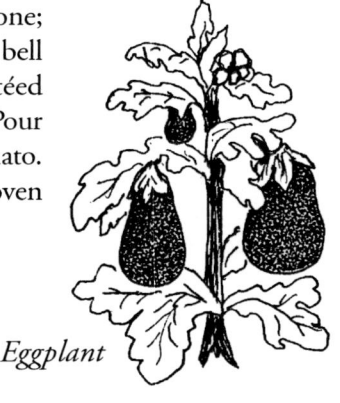

Eggplant

Jalapeño Coleslaw

2 cups thinly sliced cabbage
   (use packaged angel hair
   cabbage if you can find it)
1/2 red bell pepper, diced

1/4 cup chopped green onions
1 small ripe tomato, diced
4 or 5 pickled jalapeño slices, finely
   chopped

Combine all ingredients. Toss with oil and vinegar or Italian dressing. Season with salt and fresh ground black pepper. Serves 4 to 6.

Cabbage

Breads & Peppers

The Alamo, built 1718, San Antonio, Texas

Mama's Southern Cornbread

1-1/2 cups cornmeal
3 tablespoons flour
1 teaspoon salt
1 teaspoon baking soda

2 cups buttermilk
1 egg, beaten
3 tablespoons bacon drippings

Mix dry ingredients, taking care that the baking soda is dispersed throughout. Add buttermilk and egg, mixing well. Heat bacon drippings in a 9- to 10-inch cast-iron skillet until very hot. Add batter and bake at 450°, 20 to 25 minutes until browned on top.

Easy Monkey Bread

Great for breakfast, and so easy.

3/4 cup sugar or brown sugar
1 teaspoon cinnamon
3 cans ready-to-eat buttermilk biscuits

1 stick butter or margarine
1/2 cup each, chopped pecans and
   raisins (optional)

Mix sugar with cinnamon in a shallow bowl. Cut biscuits into quarters and roll in the sugar-cinnamon mixture. Pile in a greased and floured angel food or Bundt pan. Melt the butter in a small saucepan and add the remaining cinnamon-sugar mixture, heating until sugar is no longer grainy. Pour over biscuits and bake in a 350° oven 30 to 40 minutes. Let stand about 10 minutes, then invert onto a large plate. For additional flavor, spread 1/2 cup chopped pecans and 1/2 cup raisins among the biscuit pieces.

Texas Muffin Bread

One level teaspoon soda—now
And three good eggs you'll choose—
A little salt, one quart of meal
And some buttermilk you'll use;
Then bake it quick and serve it hot,
And when your table's spread,
No kingly food you'll find so good
As "Texas Muffin Bread."
—*from an 1895 Texas cookbook*

Ranch Biscuits

This recipe shows up often in community cookbooks and is a direct descendant of the sourdough biscuits made by the chuck-wagon cook long ago.

5 cups flour
1 teaspoon baking powder
1 teaspoon baking soda
3 tablespoons sugar
1 teaspoon salt

3/4 cup vegetable shortening
1 package dry yeast dissolved in
    1/4 cup warm (not hot) water
2 cups buttermilk

Sift dry ingredients together. Cut in shortening. Mix yeast, water, and buttermilk; add mixture to dry ingredients. Knead dough for 2 to 3 minutes. Pinch off rolls and bake on greased pan at 350° for 35 minutes. Cover unused dough and place in refrigerator. Roll out and bake like rolls or biscuits as needed. Dough will keep for up to 2 weeks.

Brazos River Cornbread

This recipe came from a Texas State Fair cookbook.

6 medium yellow crookneck squash, sliced
2 medium zucchini squash, sliced
1/2 cup onion, chopped
1 small green or red bell pepper
2 cups water
2 (8-ounce) packages Mexican cornbread mix

3 eggs
1 cup sour cream
1/3 cup vegetable oil
1 small jar, chopped pimentos
8 slices bacon, fried crisp and crumbled
2 cups grated longhorn or Cheddar cheese

(continued)

Boil first five ingredients until barely tender. Drain off excess water and mash well. In a large mixing bowl, combine cornbread mix, sour cream, oil, pimentos, and eggs. Mix well. Stir in squash mixture. Grease 8 x 8-inch square pan. Pour in 1/2 of cornbread mixture. Sprinkle all of crumbled bacon and 1-1/2 cups of cheese on mixture. Pour rest of cornbread mixture on top and sprinkle with remainder of cheese. Bake at 325° for 45 to 50 minutes.

Pig

Stage Coach Inn Hush Puppies

If you haven't ever eaten at the Stage Coach Inn in Salado, Texas and have occasion to drive I-35 near Austin, stop there for a meal. It is like entering the food twilight zone. The décor and menu are throwbacks to the 1950s. They still serve tomato aspic! Here is a recipe for their famous Hush Puppies which are served with the aspic.

2 cups white cornmeal	1 teaspoon salt
1 tablespoon baking powder	1/4 cup butter
3 tablespoons sugar	Oil for frying

Combine the cornmeal, baking powder, sugar, and salt. Slowly add dry mixture to 3-1/2 cups of boiling water, stirring as you add. As soon as the mixture is smooth, remove from heat. Stir in butter, mixing well. Set aside to cool. When able to handle, form into finger shaped rolls. Fry in 2 to 3 inches hot oil until golden brown. Drain on paper towels.

West Texas Cornbread

Corn

2 eggs
1/3 cup salad oil
1 cup sour cream
1 cup yellow cornmeal
1 cup cream-style corn
3 teaspoons baking powder
1/2 to 1 cup grated Cheddar cheese

1 (4-ounce) can chopped green chilies
   or jalapeños

Mix all ingredients well and bake in greased iron skillet which has been pre-heated in a hot (400°) oven. (Batter should sizzle when poured into the pan.) Bake 30 to 40 minutes, until browned on top. Remove cornbread from pan immediately.

Crisp Stuffed Jalapeños

This is the ultimate popper; more work to make, but by far the best tasting. Serve with a creamy avocado dipping sauce. Just try to eat only one! Great with frozen Margaritas or Mexican dark beer.

2 cups chopped, cooked chicken
1/4 cup salsa or picante sauce

Breading ingredients:
1 cup cracker meal
1 cup flour
2 eggs

12 medium-sized fresh jalapeño peppers
3 tablespoons finely chopped onion

1 cup milk
1/4 teaspoon salt
1/4 teaspoon pepper

(continued)

In a small bowl, mix chopped chicken with onions, salsa or picante sauce. It should moisten the chicken just enough for it to hold together.

With a sharp knife, make a slit along the side of each jalapeño, leaving the stems intact. Remove seeds if desired. Stuff peppers full of the chicken mixture.

Prepare the breading mixture:
Mix cracker meal and flour together in a shallow bowl. Beat eggs, milk, salt, and pepper together in another bowl. Dip stuffed peppers in egg mixture, then in cracker meal. Repeat procedure. Set on waxed paper to dry for at least 10 minutes. Deep-fry until golden brown. Drain on absorbent paper towels.

Note: The breading will stick better if poppers are placed in freezer for 1 hour before frying.

Tuna Jalapeño Poppers

1 (6 ounce) can tuna, well drained
2 to 3 tablespoons finely chopped
 onion
2 to 3 tablespoons mayonnaise
Salt and pepper to taste
Chopped cilantro, small amount
 (optional)

jalapeños

10 to 12 whole, canned jalapeños,
 split lengthwise, with seeds
 removed, drained on paper towels

Mix tuna, onion, mayonnaise, salt and pepper, and cilantro. Place a tablespoon of the tuna mixture on each half pepper. This recipe is great to make ahead, as it can be covered and refrigerated until ready to serve.

Bacon-Cheddar Poppers

1 (12-ounce) block Cheddar or
   Cheddar/Jack cheese
6 large fresh jalapeño peppers, seeded and sliced in half lengthwise

6 slices of bacon, cut in half

Preheat oven to 375°. Cut cheese into slices long enough to fit inside the pepper halves. Fill the pepper halves with slices of cheese. Lay the half bacon slices lengthwise over the top of the cheese. Place on greased baking sheet and bake about 20 to 30 minutes until pepper is cooked. Turn oven to broil to brown bacon tops, cooking for 2 to 3 minutes.

These poppers are also great cooked on the barbeque grill. Just place on edge of grill away from hottest part of fire and let cook about 25 to 30 minutes.

Sweet Stuff

Texas oranges

Rio Grande Valley Grapefruit Cake

1-1/2 cups sifted cake flour
3/4 cup sugar
1-1/2 teaspoons baking powder
1/2 teaspoon salt
1/4 cup water

1/4 cup salad oil
3 eggs, separated
3 tablespoons grapefruit juice
1/2 teaspoon grated lemon rind
1/4 teaspoon cream of tartar

Sift flour, sugar, baking powder, and salt into a large bowl. Make a "hole" in the center of the flour mixture and add water, oil, egg yolks, grapefruit juice, and lemon rind. Mix well and then beat thoroughly until smooth. In clean glass bowl, beat egg whites and the cream of tartar until stiff but not dry. Fold batter mixture into beaten egg whites until blended; do not stir mixture. Pour into a greased 9-inch layer cake pan. Bake in moderate oven (350°) for 25 to 30 minutes until done; cake springs back when lightly touched on top with finger. Remove from oven and let cool 10 minutes. Run spatula around edge of pan and invert pan to place cake on rack to cool more.

When cool, cut through cake horizontally with a serrated knife to make two layers. Frost with the following Grapefruit Cream Cheese Icing and garnish with grapefruit sections.

Grapefruit Cream Cheese Icing

2 (3-ounce) packages cream cheese
1 teaspoon grated lemon rind
3 tablespoons lemon juice
3 cups powdered sugar
2 cups grapefruit sections or 1 can grapefruit sections (place grapefruit sections on paper towels to drain)
Yellow or red food coloring

(continued)

Beat cream cheese until soft and fluffy; add lemon rind, juice, and powdered sugar. Crush sufficient grapefruit sections to make 1 tablespoon of juice or enough juice to make soft frosting. Blend thoroughly. Lightly tint icing with yellow or red food coloring, depending on whether the grapefruit sections are white or ruby.

To assemble cake:
Spread icing on bottom layer and top with grapefruit sections. Cover with second layer, then frost top and sides. Garnish with more grapefruit sections on top. (You can also add a few maraschino cherries for more color.)

Historic Recipe for a Happy Day

Into each day put:
4 parts each of faith, patience, and courage
3 parts of work (if omitted, the flavor is spoiled),
4 parts each of hope and fidelity
5 parts of kindness, picking off all specks of pettiness and littleness
1 part rest (if omitted, the flavor is impaired)
Pinch of folly, 2 parts prayer and meditation
1 well-selected resolution

—from a historic Texas cookbook

Pecan Pie

Early pecan pies called for using molasses or sorghum syrup. Then Karo™ brand corn syrup put a pecan recipe on the labels of its bottles. This quickly became the preferred recipe. In fact, in 1920 cookbooks called the pie "Karo™ Pie." Here is this old favorite, easy to make and sure to please.

1 cup pecan halves	1 teaspoon vanilla
1 unbaked 9-inch pie shell	1-1/4 cups dark corn syrup
3 eggs	1 cup sugar
2 tablespoons melted butter	1 tablespoon flour

Arrange nuts in pie shell. Beat eggs; add melted butter, vanilla, corn syrup, sugar, and flour. Mix well and pour over pecans in pie shell. Bake in 350° oven 45 minutes. Serve with whipped cream topping or a little vanilla ice cream on the side.

Pecan Pie Squares

2 cups brown sugar
3/4 cup butter

2 cups all-purpose flour

Mix these three ingredients and press into a 13 x 15-inch jellyroll pan. Bake 18 to 20 minutes in 350° oven. Remove from oven.

Combine:
3 slightly beaten eggs
1 cup dark Karo™ syrup
1 cup sugar
1-1/2 cups chopped pecans

1 tablespoon flour
1/2 teaspoon salt
1/2 teaspoon vanilla

Mix ingredients well. Spread over baked crust, return to oven, and bake 20 minutes longer. Cool and cut into squares. Makes 3 dozen.

Cherry Dumplings

Pie crust dough, either puchased
or make your own
2 cans sour pie cherries,
drained, reserve juice

Sugar
Butter

Roll out pie dough very thin and cut into triangles. Place two tablespoons cherries in center of triangle, top with three tablespoons of sugar. Fold over and place dumpling in baking dish. Continue making dumplings and placing in dish. Pour drained reserved cherry juice around the dumplings until it goes about half way up side of dish. Place a piece of butter on top of each dumpling and sprinkle more sugar on dumplings. Bake in 350° oven for 45 minutes.

Pastel de Tres Leches (Three Milks Cake)

This cake has been popular in Nicaragua, Guatemala, and Southern Mexico for many years. Some food experts say the recipe was originally printed on the label of canned milk sold in those regions. Latin-American immigrants brought the recipe to Texas, and Texans fell in love with its rich, creamy flavor. It is now popular dessert fare in Mexican restaurants from El Paso to Texarkana.

To enjoy the full favor of this delicious cake, it is best served cold. Any remaining cake should be kept in the refrigerator.

For cake:

6 eggs, separated
2 cups sugar
2 teaspoons vanilla (Mexican is best)
2 cups flour
3 teaspoons baking powder
1/2 cup milk

(continued)

For Three Milks sauce: (mix together)
1 cup evaporated milk
1 cup sweetened condensed milk

1 cup heavy cream or Mexican Crema

For topping:
2 egg whites
1-1/2 cups sugar
1/8 teaspoon salt

1/3 cup water
2 tablespoons white corn syrup
2 teaspoons vanilla

Make cake:
Beat egg whites until peaks form. Add sugar gradually, then add yolks and vanilla, beating for 3 minutes. Sift flour and baking powder together and add to egg mixture alternately with milk. Pour into a well-greased 9 x 13-inch pan. Bake at 350° for 30 to 40 minutes until top springs back when touched. Remove from

oven and cool about 10 minutes. Remove top crust from cake, leaving a ridge around the edge of the cake to hold the sauce. Punch holes in cake with toothpick. Pour the Three Milks sauce over the warm cake and place in refrigerator at least 2 hours until cool.

To make topping:
Mix all topping ingredients in top of double boiler. Beat the mixture constantly while cooking over the hot water, about 7 to 10 minutes or until soft peaks form. Cover cake with frosting.

To serve:
Keep cake in refrigerator. Cut into slices to serve. Garnish with maraschino cherries or fresh, sliced strawberries.

Mandarin Orange Cake

1 yellow cake mix
4 eggs

2/3 cup oil
1 (11-ounce) can mandarin oranges, undrained

Mix ingredients beating for 3 to 5 minutes. Pour into 9 x 13-inch baking pan greased and floured. Bake for 25 to 30 minutes at 350°. Remove from oven and allow to cool.

Icing:
1 large (20-ounce) can crushed pineapple, drained

1 (16-ounce) carton Cool Whip™
1 (6-ounce) package instant vanilla or French vanilla pudding

Mix ingredients, beating well. Spread over cake. Chill cake 2 to 3 hours, or overnight before serving. Keep cake covered and refrigerated.

Red Velvet Cake

Many people think the Red Velvet Cake has southern origins because it is so popular in the South. This cake actually originated in New York City at the Waldorf-Astoria Hotel. This famous cake spawned an urban myth that began circulating sometime during the 1940s.

The story goes like this: A woman was staying at the elegant Waldorf and after sampling the cake in the dining room, she requested the recipe. The next day when she went to check out of the hotel, $100 had been added to her bill for the cost of the recipe. The angry woman, with revenge in mind, started handing out the recipe, along with her story everywhere she went, asking that others pass the recipe and the story on. Sometime during the 1960s, this tale "morphed" into a cookie recipe from Neiman Marcus in Dallas, and the price rose to $250 that was charged to the irate customer's credit card. Whatever the recipe's origin, it makes a stunning cake. The white icing conceals the bright red insides until the spectacular moment when the first slice is removed from the cake. This cake with its red color is perfect for Christmas, Valentine's Day, and with a little adjustment for a crimson color, Texas A&M football parties. I have found hundreds of Red Velvet Cake recipes, all with minor variations. Here is a recipe that I have used many times. I prefer the cream cheese frosting over the cooked icing that usually goes with the cake. You can vary the shade of red by adding less cake coloring. One bottle of red food coloring, which is the equivalent of 2 tablespoons, will make a bright pink cake. Two bottles, which is the equivalent of 4 tablespoons, give the cake its popular deep red color.

The Famous Red Velvet Cake

1/2 cup Crisco™ shortening
1-1/2 cups sugar
1 teaspoon vanilla
2 eggs
3 tablespoons cocoa
2 (1-ounce) bottles of red food coloring
2-1/2 cups sifted cake flour
1 cup buttermilk
1 teaspoon baking powder
1 tablespoon white vinegar
1 teaspoon salt

Cream shortening and sugar until light; add the vanilla and mix well. Add eggs, one at a time, beating after each addition. Make a paste of the cocoa and the red food coloring. Add to the creamed mixture. Add flour and buttermilk alternately, mixing well after each addition. Mix the baking powder, salt, and vinegar in a small

(continued)

bowl and add to the batter. Blend well. Bake in two or three 9-inch baking pans that have been greased and lined with waxed paper or baking parchment. Bake 20 to 25 minutes at 350°. Remove pans from oven and let stand for 5 minutes, then turn cakes out on racks to cool.

Frosting

2 (3-ounce) packages cream cheese, softened
1 teaspoon vanilla

6 tablespoons butter, softened
3 cups powdered sugar, sifted

Blend all ingredients until smooth. Spread between layers and on tops and sides of the cooled cake. If frosting is too stiff, thin with a little milk.

Jalapeño Café's Margarita Ice Box Pie

Here is an easy-to-make recipe I developed using a prepared no-bake pie shell, whipped dessert topping, and frozen Margarita mix. Make this pie at least 4 to 5 hours before serving to give it time to set in the refrigerator until firm.

1 prepared graham cracker pie shell (large size)
1/2 cup water
2 packets plain gelatin
1 (10-ounce) can Bacardi™ Frozen Lime (Margarita) Mix
4 tablespoons sugar
3 drops green food coloring or enough to tint the filling
1/4 cup tequila
1 tablespoon Triple Sec™ liquor
1 (12-ounce) carton whipped dessert topping
Grated peel of 1 lime

(continued)

Place pie shell in freezer to chill at least 2 hours before making filling (a cold shell will make the pie set more quickly).

Place water in small bowl and heat to boiling in microwave, about 1-1/2 minutes. Add the plain gelatin to the water and stir until completely dissolved.

In large bowl, combine the Margarita mix, sugar, and food coloring; add the gelatin mixture and stir well. Place the mixture in the refrigerator about 30 to 45 minutes to chill. It should be just slightly thickened.

Add the tequila and Triple Sec™. Next add the whipped topping to the Margarita mixture (reserve about 1 cup of topping to garnish pie). Use whisk or electric mixer to incorporate the Margarita mixture into the whipped topping. Beat about 2 minutes until thoroughly combined and uniform in color.

Pour mixture into the pie shell. Place pie in refrigerator to chill at least 2 to 3 hours. Pie will set firm. Before serving, spoon remaining topping onto center of pie and garnish with the grated lime peel.

Peggy's Banana Cake with Lemon Pecan Icing

My sister-in-law, Jeanette Bullard, gave me this recipe in the 1960s. I don't know Peggy, but I have made her cake many times.

2-1/4 cups cake flour	1-1/2 cups sugar
1/2 teaspoon baking powder	2 eggs
3/4 teaspoon soda	1 cup mashed ripe bananas
1/2 teaspoon salt	1 teaspoon vanilla
1/2 cup butter	1/4 cup buttermilk (or plain yogurt)

Have ingredients at room temperature and preheat oven to 350°. Grease and flour two or three 9-inch cake pans. (I always line my cake pans with a circle of waxed paper.)

(continued)

Sift the flour with the baking powder, soda, and salt, and set aside. In a large mixing bowl, cream the butter, then add the sugar and continue creaming until mixture is light and fluffy. Beat in eggs, one at a time. Mix the bananas with the vanilla and buttermilk.

Add the flour mixture to the butter mixture in about 3 parts, alternating with the banana mixture. Stir the batter until smooth after each addition. Pour even amounts of the batter in each pan and bake for 25 to 30 minutes until done. Remove from oven, cool 5 minutes, then turn out on rack to cool.

To assemble, ice bottom layer, arrange a layer of sliced bananas over icing, then place next layer on top (if three layers) and repeat. Then place top layer on and ice top and sides of cake. Sprinkle with 1/4 cup of reserved pecans listed in the icing recipe.

Lemon Pecan Icing recipe follows.

Lemon Pecan Icing

2 (3-ounce) packages cream cheese
3 tablespoons butter
3 to 4 tablespoons lemon juice
1 cup chopped toasted pecans
1/8 teaspoon salt
1 (1 pound) box of confectioner's sugar sifted

In medium-size bowl, mix cream cheese, butter, and salt. Add confectioner's sugar and enough lemon juice to make an icing of creamy spreading consistency. Beat icing until smooth, and then add toasted pecans (reserve 1/4 cup nuts for garnish), mixing well.

To toast pecans:
Place nuts on baking pan and bake in 325° oven about 12 minutes or until lightly browned, stirring often to prevent burning. Cool before using.

Seven Minute Icing

A prize-winning recipe of the 1939 New York World's Fair.

2 egg whites	1-1/2 cups sugar
2 tablespoons white Karo™ syrup	1/2 cup water
Dash salt	1 teaspoon vanilla

Place all ingredients except vanilla in top of double boiler. Mix thoroughly. Cook over high heat, beating constantly until mixture forms peaks (7 minutes). Remove from heat, add vanilla, and beat until of spreading consistency.

Texarkana Chocolate Syrup Cake

Texarkana is a city in two states, Texas and Arkansas. Arkansas is famous for its chocolate gravy and this cake has the same syrupy flavor, sure to suit the citizens of both sections of the city.

1 cup sugar
2 sticks (1 cup) butter, melted
4 eggs
1 cup self-rising flour
1 (16-ounce) can chocolate syrup
1 teaspoon vanilla

Mix all ingredients in the order given, stirring well after each addition. When all are added, beat for two minutes. Pour into greased 9 x 13-inch baking dish. Bake for 20 minutes at 350°.

Frosting:

1 stick butter (1/2 cup)

1 cup sugar

1/2 cup chocolate chips

1/3 cup evaporated milk

1/2 cup chopped pecans

Combine all ingredients in a sauce pan and simmer slowly. Let mixture come to a boil, stirring constantly for several minutes. Pour over cake. Let stand until cool.

Mud Hens

1/2 cup butter
1 cup brown sugar
1/2 teaspoon salt
1-1/2 cups flour
1 teaspoon baking powder

1 teaspoon vanilla
2 eggs
1/2 cup chopped pecans
1 cup light brown sugar

Cream butter and sugar. Sift together salt, flour, and baking powder. Add to butter mixture, then add vanilla. Separate one of the eggs and save the white. Add the whole egg and yolk to mixture and blend. Spread in buttered shallow baking pan to a depth of 1/2-inch thick. Sprinkle with the chopped nuts, pressing in slightly. Beat reserved egg white together with light brown sugar. Spread over the top of the mixture in the pan. Bake 30 minutes at 350°. Cut into squares while warm.

Fredrickburg Chocolate Chewies

3 cups firmly packed
confectioner's sugar
7 tablespoons leveled and packed
cocoa (1/2 cup minus 1
tablespoon)

2 tablespoons all-purpose flour
3 egg whites
2 cups (8-ounces) finely chopped
pecans

Preheat oven to 350°. Line two baking sheets with parchment paper. In a medium-size mixing bowl, combine the sugar, cocoa, and flour. Add the egg whites and beat at high speed for 1 minute. Stir in the pecans. Using 1-1/2 tablespoons of batter for each, drop the cookies 2 inches apart onto the baking sheets. Press the tops of the cookies to lightly flatten.

Bake for 15 minutes. Let the cookies cool on the parchment paper before removing them. Store in an airtight container. Makes 2 dozen cookies.

Pineapple Drop Cookies

1/2 cup butter or shortening
1/2 cup white sugar
1/2 cup brown sugar
1 egg, beaten
1/2 cup well drained crushed pineapple

2 cups flour
1 teaspoon baking powder
1/4 teaspoon salt
1/4 teaspoon baking soda
1 teaspoon vanilla
1 cup chopped pecans

Cream butter and sugars well. Add egg and pineapple, mixing well. Sift dry ingredients and add to creamed mixture. Add vanilla and blend in nuts by hand. Chill mixture for 20 minutes. Drop by level teaspoonful onto greased baking sheets. Bake 8 to 10 minutes in 375° oven or until lightly browned.

Fairy Pie

This old San Antonio recipe makes an elegant dessert.

1/2 cup butter
1/2 cup granulated sugar
4 egg yolks, beaten until light
1/2 cup sifted flour

4 tablespoons milk
2 tablespoons flour, sifted with
    1 teaspoon baking powder

Meringue:
4 egg whites, beaten with a pinch
    of salt
1 cup granulated sugar

1 teaspoon vanilla
Finely chopped nuts

Cream butter and sugar, add egg yolks and mix well. Add flour and milk alternately and, finally, add the baking powder-flour mixture. Turn into two well-greased and floured layer cake pans.

Add salt to egg whites, beat until stiff. Gradually add the sugar and mix in flavoring. Pile half meringue on each of the uncooked layers. Bake in moderate oven (350°) for 20 to 25 minutes. Allow to cool in pans, then invert one layer, cover with whipped cream and seasonal berries. Place other layer meringue side up.

SOPAPILLAS

This fried pastry is a popular dessert on Mexican restaurant menus. The pastries puff up like little pillows while frying, hence the name. A sopapilla topped with honey with a scoop of cinnamon ice cream on the side is a perfect ending to a hot chili dinner.

This recipe is a standard in Texas community cookbooks, usually listed in the section on Tex-Mex or Mexican cooking. I found this recipe in Texas cookbooks so many times that I stopped counting. It is so simple to make that recipe variations are rare and mostly deal with the measurements. Here is a recipe that will make a large enough batch to feed six to eight people.

Sopapillas

3 cups flour
2 teaspoons baking powder
1 teaspoon salt

2 tablespoons shortening
1 cup milk
Salad oil (for frying)

Sift flour, baking powder, and salt into bowl. Cut in shortening until mixture resembles coarse meal. Add enough milk to make a thick, stiff dough. Roll out to a 1/4 inch thickness and cut into 3-inch squares. Fry in hot oil until brown on one side; turn and brown on other side. Drain on paper towels.

Serve warm, dusted with powdered sugar or cinnamon-sugar mixture. Honey is usually served with this dessert.

Texas Buttermilk Pie

1-1/2 cups sugar
3 tablespoons flour
2 eggs, well beaten
1/2 cup butter, melted

1 cup buttermilk
1 teaspoon vanilla
1/2 teaspoon nutmeg
1 unbaked 9-inch pie shell

In large bowl, combine sugar and flour, mixing well. Stir in eggs. Add melted butter and buttermilk. Add vanilla and nutmeg, stirring to mix. Pour into pie shell and bake at 425° for 10 minutes. Reduce heat to 350° and bake 30 to 35 minutes more.

Holiday Rum Cake

This recipe was given to me by one of my Houston cooking friends.

2 cups water
2 cups sugar
4 eggs
2 cups chopped dried fruit
1 teaspoon baking soda

2-3/4 cups flour
1 teaspoon vanilla
1 cup chopped pecans or walnuts
1/4 cup grape juice
1 bottle dark rum

First, sample the rum to check for freshness and flavor.

(continued)

Take a large bowl. Check the rum again. To be sure it is of the highest quality, pour one level cup of rum and drink. Repeat. Turn on electric mixer; beat the butter in the fluffy bowl. Add half of the sugar and heat, I mean beat, again.

Make sure the rum is OK. Cry another tup. Turn off the mixer. Add the flour leggs to the bowl and chuck in the cup of dried druit. Mix on the burner, no I mean the turner. If the dried druit gets stuck in the beaterers, pry it loose with a drewscriver. Sample the rum for tonsisticity. Now, sift two cups of salt. Or something. Who cares? Check the rum.

Now, sift the grape juice and strain your nuts. Add one table. Spoon. Of sugar . . . or something . . . whatever you can find.

Grease the oven. Turn cake pan to 350°. Don't forget to beat off the turner. Throw bowl out the window. Check the rum again and go to bed.

Drinks

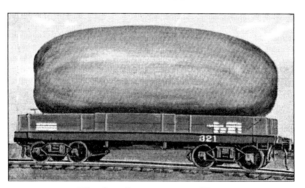

The kind we grow in Texas

Classic Margarita

In a cocktail shaker with cracked ice:

Juice of 1/2 lime
1 ounce tequila
Shaved ice

1/2 ounce Triple Sec™ or
Cointreau™

Shake and strain into a chilled Margarita or champagne glass that has been edged with salt.

Note: To edge glass with salt, rub the rim of the glass with a piece of lime, then dip and turn the glass in a saucer of salt. Shake slightly to remove excess.

Tower Club Blue Margarita

The Tower Club in Dallas is famous for its many different Margaritas. This one is the most spectacular.

1-1/2 ounces tequila
3/4 ounce Triple Sec™ or Cointreau™
4 ounces sweet-and-sour mix
Dash simple syrup

Dash Rose's Lime Juice™
Dash Grand Marnier™
1/2 ounce Blue Curaçao™
Juice of half a fresh orange

Combine all ingredients in a cocktail shaker. Shake well and pour drink through a strainer into a chilled stemmed glass. Add ice and garnish with lime slice.

Easy Frozen Margaritas

1 (6-ounce) can frozen limeade
    concentrate
6 ounces tequila
2 ounces Triple Sec™
    (or Cointreau™)

6 ounces lemon-lime soda
5 cups crushed ice
Lime slices
Salt

Mix limeade concentrate, tequila, Triple Sec™, and lemon-lime soda in pitcher. Place crushed ice in blender; add limeade mixture. Blend until mixture is smooth and slushy. Pour into chilled glasses that have the rim salted by rubbing with a lime slice, then dipping in salt. Garnish drinks with lime slices.

Frozen Watermelon Margarita

3 cups watermelon juice
3/4 cup tequila
1/3 cup Triple Sec™
1/3 cup fresh lime juice
Lime wedges

Make ahead: Remove seeds and process watermelon for yield of 3 cups juice. Pour the watermelon juice into ice trays and freeze until firm.

Make Margaritas: Transfer 2/3 of the frozen melon cubes to a blender; add liquor and lime juice. Blend until almost smooth. Add the remaining cubes and blend until smooth. Serves 4.

To serve: Pour into chilled glasses that have been prepared by rubbing edges with lime, then dipping in salt. Colored sugar can also be used for a sweeter and more colorful drink.

"Rootin' Tootin'" Wham

6 parts light rum   2 parts lime juice   1 part grenadine

Combine all ingredients in a cocktail shaker. Add crushed ice and shake well. Serves 4.

Hot Dr. Pepper™—A True Texas Drink

Here is the recipe for this old Texas favorite, simple to make and easy to expand the proportion.

Heat 12 ounces of Dr. Pepper™ in a saucepan until hot with bubbles rising to the top. Add two thin slices of lemon. Pour into cups or mugs. Serves 2.

Old-fashioned (Texas) Peach Slush

The Peach Fuzzy recipe is the blender-made version of an old southern favorite, Peach Slush. The hill country of central Texas produces some of the finest peaches in the United States, and it is only natural that the old recipe for Peach Slush would be modified to suit a Texan's taste. The recipe originated long before blenders and food processors. The secret to making drinks using peaches is to have very ripe fruit.

1/2 ripe peach, peeled	1 heaping teaspoon sugar
2 jiggers whiskey	Crushed ice

Mash together peach and sugar until sugar is dissolved; add whiskey and stir well. Fill large (12-ounce) glass with crushed ice. Pour peach mixture over the ice, stirring once or twice. Makes 1 drink.

Texas Bellini

Thanks to Judith Aldridge of Trophy Club, Texas, for this recipe for a frozen version of the Italian peach cocktail.

Fill a blender half-full with ice cubes and add:

2 large or 3 medium-sized *ripe* peaches, peeled, seeds removed

2 tablespoons lemon juice
3/4 cup Asti Spumante™

Blend until ingredients are puréed into a frozen mixture. Serve in chilled champagne glasses.

Cerveza Roja (Red Beer)

Cerveza Roja *or Red Beer is an old, working man's cure for a hangover. It consists of good lager mixed with chilled tomato juice. It has been called Tomato Beer, Red Eye, Red Dog, and Red Rooster. In America, this drink enjoyed a surge in popularity during the 1950s, and many brewing companies bottled it in quart bottles made of ruby red glass. The red glass beer bottles are avidly sought by collectors today. Here's a recipe with a little heat.*

1 (5.5 ounce) can tomato juice
Pinch of cayenne pepper
Dash Tabasco™ sauce
Dash of seasoning salt
1 (12-ounce) can beer

Pour tomato juice into chilled 16-ounce beer mug. Add seasonings and mix. Pour in beer and stir slightly to mix.

New Mexico-style Coffee

The Chimayo Restaurant in Chimayo, New Mexico, popularized this after-dinner coffee made with Kahlúa™ and tequila. The drink first appeared on its menu in the 1960s.

1 cup fresh-brewed coffee
1 ounce Kahlúa™

1 ounce tequila
Whipped cream

Pour coffee into tall mug. Add Kahlúa™ and tequila, stirring slightly. Top with a dollop of whipped cream and serve immediately.

Mexican Coffee

1 cup fresh brewed coffee
Dash of cinnamon

1 ounce Kahlúa™
Whipped cream

Pour coffee into a tall mug; add cinnamon and Kahlúa™ and mix slightly. Top with a little whipped cream and serve immediately.

Iced Mexican Coffee

8 ounces fresh-brewed extra-strong coffee
2 tablespoons chocolate syrup

2 ounces Kahlúa™
2 tablespoons sugar
2 tablespoons cream or half-and-half

Mix ingredients and pour into two 16-ounce glasses filled with crushed ice. Serve immediately.

COOKOFFS in TEXAS

Cookoffs are social events in which competitors prepare their own recipes for a particular dish, and submit it to a panel of judges for taste testing. The judges use a blind selection process to award a prize for the best recipe. In Texas, cookoffs take place almost year-round throughout the state.

Two sanctioning organizations provide rules and a membership structure for chili and barbeque cookoffs. The Chili Appreciation Society International (CASI) and the Central Texas Barbeque Association (CTBA) were formed to establish fair and equal guidelines for all competitive cookoffs.

A sampling of events is listed here. Check websites or contact the chamber of commerce of the hosting city to confirm dates and times of events, as they vary from year to year.

Austin
Star of Texas Fair & Rodeo

Bay City
Matagorda County Fair Barbecue Cook-Off

Galveston
Annual World Wild Game Championship and Barbeque Cook-Off

Grand Prairie
Prairie Dog Chili Cook-Off & World Championship Pickled Egg Eating

Houston
Shoulda Been A Cowboy Association BBQ Cook-Off

Johnson City
Texas Men's State Chili Championship & Texas Men's State BBQ Championship

Lockhart
Annual Chisholm Trail Roundup BBQ

Seguin
Texas Ladies State Chili Championship

Sulphur Springs
Annual World Champion Hopkins County Stew Contest

Sweetwater
Sweetwater Jaycee's Annual Brisket/Chili Cook-Off, Salsa Cook-Off, & Dessert Cook-off

Terlingua
Terlingua International Chili Championship

Woodland
Annual Woodland Dynamite Chili Cook-Off

Index of Recipes

Appetizers 5–22

Pico de Gallo One 6

Pico de Gallo Two 6

Easy Skillet Fajitas 7

Prairie Fire One 9

Prairie Fire Two 10

Lady Bird's Cheese Wafers 11

Old-fashioned Cheese Dollars 12

Armadillo Eggs 13

GUACAMOLE 14

Perfect Guacamole 15

Poo Poos 16

Guacamole Dip 17

Texas Caviar 18

Black-Eyed Pea Dip or Salad 20

Jalapeño Café Snack Mix 22

**Salads, Sauces, Soups &
Main Dishes** 23–97

Frito™ Pie 24

Frito™ Enchilada Pie 25

Oven Barbeque Brisket 26

A Bowl of Red 28	Split Pea Soup–Slow Cooker 48
Pioneer Jailhouse Chili 29	**Chicken** 50
Classic Texas Chili 31	Cherokee Chicken 51
Pinto Beans 33	Cerise Chicken 52
Charro Beans 34	King Ranch Chicken 54
Jalapeño Café Enchilada Casserole .. 36	Squash Dressing 57
Pinto Bean Soup 38	Sonora Chicken Pie 58
Frijoles Refritos 40	**Sugar Frying** 60
Maggie's Hot Cheese Toasts 41	Sugar-fried Chicken 61
Sweet and Spicy Shrimp 42	Sugar-browned Potatoes 63
Texas Shrimp Gumbo 44	**Cranberries** 64
Baked Potato Chowder 46	Double Cranberry Relish 65

Cranberry Christmas Punch 66	South Dallas Short Ribs 87
Cranberry Catsup 67	Macaroni and Cheese Mexicana 89
Historic Texas Cookbook Advice ... 69	Cabbage Tamales 91
TEX-MEX ENCHILADS & TACOS ... 70	Texas Goulash 93
Texas Red Chili Sauce 71	Eggplant Casserole 95
Sour Cream Chicken Enchiladas 73	Jalapeño Coleslaw 97
Beef Enchiladas 77	
Cheese Enchiladas 78	**Breads and Peppers** **98–110**
230 Pound Psalm 80	Mama's Southern Cornbread 99
Ham Tacos 81	Easy Monkey Bread 100
Sweet Potato Custard 84	Texas Muffin Bread 101
East Texas Slow Oven Stew 85	Ranch Biscuits 102

Brazos River Cornbread 103
Stage Coach Inn Hush Puppies ... 105
West Texas Cornbread 106
Crisp Stuffed Jalapeños 107
Tuna Jalapeño Poppers............ 109
Bacon-Cheddar Poppers 110

Sweet Stuff **111–144**
Grapefruit Cake 112
Grapefruit Cream Cheese Icing ... 113
Historic Recipe for a Happy Day ... 115
Pecan Pie 116

Pecan Pie Squares 117
Cherry Dumplings................. 118
Pastel de Tres Leches 119
Mandarin Orange Cake 122
RED VELVET CAKE 123
The Famous Red Velvet Cake ... 125
Margarita Ice Box Pie 127
Peggy's Banana Cake 129
Lemon Pecan Icing 131
Seven Minute Icing................ 132
Texarkana Chocolate Syrup
   Cake 133

Mud Hens 135

Fredrickburg Chocolate
   Chewies........................... 136

Pineapple Drop Cookies 137

Fairy Pie 138

SOPAPILLAS 140

Sopapillas 141

Texas Buttermilk Pie 142

Holiday Rum Cake 143

Drinks **145–155**

Classic Margarita 146

Tower Club Blue Margarita 147

Easy Frozen Margarita 148

Frozen Watermelon Margarita 149

"Rootin' Tootin'" Wham.......... 150

Hot Dr. Pepper™ 150

Old-fashioned Peach Slush 151

Texas Bellini 152

Cerveza Roja (Red Beer) 153

New Mexico-style Coffee 154

Mexican Coffee..................... 155

Iced Mexican Coffee 155

BOOKS BY MAIL Stocking Stuffers POSTPAID You may mix titles. One book for $10.95; two for $16; three for $23; four for $28; twelve for $75. *(Prices subject to change.)* Please call 1-800-728-9998.

- Texas Cookoff (this book)
- Tales of Texas Tables
- License To Cook Texas Style
- Æbleskiver and More (Danish)
- Dandy Dutch Recipes
- Dutch Style Recipes
- Dear Danish Recipes
- Fine Finnish Foods
- German Style Recipes
- Great German Recipes
- Norwegian Recipes
- Scandinavian Holiday Recipes
- Scandinavian Smorgasbord Recipes
- Scandinavian Sweet Treats
- Splendid Swedish Recipes
- Time-Honored Norwegian Recipes
- Slavic Specialties
- Pleasing Polish Recipes
- Cherished Czech Recipes
- Czech & Slovak Kolaches & Sweet Treats
- Quality Dumpling Recipes
- Amish Mennonite Recipes & Traditions
- Recipes from Ireland
- Savory Scottish Recipes
- Ukrainian Recipes

Complete Catalog of more titles $2.50

Stewing in Texas $18.95.
2 for $25.00 Postpaid.
Recipes Sizzling in Texas History,
A Cookbook War, and More
6x9", 128 pages with 16 color pages.

PENFIELD BOOKS • 215 BROWN STREET • IOWA CITY, IA 52245-5801 • WWW.PENFIELDBOOKS.COM